DATA IN YOUR WORLD

EXPLORING OUR SCHOOLS

Courtney Koestler and
Mathew Felton-Koestler

Rourke
Educational Media

A Division of
Carson
Dellosa
Education

BEFORE AND DURING READING ACTIVITIES

Before Reading: *Building Background Knowledge and Vocabulary*

Building background knowledge can help children process new information and build upon what they already know. Before reading a book, it is important to tap into what children already know about the topic. This will help them develop their vocabulary and increase their reading comprehension.

Questions and Activities to Build Background Knowledge:

1. Look at the front cover of the book and read the title. What do you think this book will be about?
2. What do you already know about this topic?
3. Take a book walk and skim the pages. Look at the table of contents, photographs, captions, and bold words. Did these text features give you any information or predictions about what you will read in this book?

Vocabulary: *Vocabulary Is Key to Reading Comprehension*

Use the following directions to prompt a conversation about each word.

- Read the vocabulary words.
- What comes to mind when you see each word?
- What do you think each word means?

Vocabulary Words:
- bias
- biracial
- connectivity
- diversity
- injustice
- projection
- racism
- refute
- represent
- student body
- trends
- tuition

During Reading: *Reading for Meaning and Understanding*

To achieve deep comprehension of a book, children are encouraged to use close reading strategies. During reading, it is important to have children stop and make connections. These connections result in deeper analysis and understanding of a book.

 Close Reading a Text

During reading, have children stop and talk about the following:

- Any confusing parts
- Any unknown words
- Text to text, text to self, text to world connections
- The main idea in each chapter or heading

Encourage children to use context clues to determine the meaning of any unknown words. These strategies will help children learn to analyze the text more thoroughly as they read.

When you are finished reading this book, turn to the next-to-last page for **Text-Dependent Questions** and an **Extension Activity**.

Table of Contents

What Is Data and Why Is It Important?

Data is all around us, and it is an important part of our society. What is data? Simply put, data is facts and statistics that are collected to be organized and analyzed. Once organized and analyzed, it becomes information that teaches us about our world.

Is Data Singular or Plural?

Over the years, scientists have treated the word *data* as plural, and they would write "These data show that ..." However, today, it's increasingly common to treat *data* as singular, such as, "This data shows that ...," which is what we will do in this book.

Let's connect data to our lives by looking at examples in our world.

Scores on State Standardized Tests

English Language Arts | Math

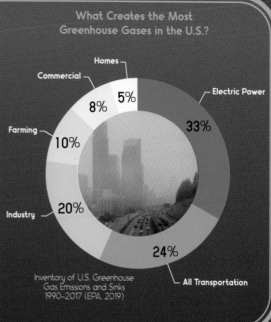

What Creates the Most Greenhouse Gases in the U.S.?

Homes — 5%
Commercial — 8%
Electric Power — 33%
Farming — 10%
Industry — 20%
All Transportation — 24%

Inventory of U.S. Greenhouse Gas Emissions and Sinks 1990-2017 (EPA, 2019)

Data and Information

Data	Information
Scores on State Standardized Tests	Student test scores for five years are compared to see if scores are increasing
What Creates the Most Greenhouse Gases in the U.S.?	Carbon emissions are measured to show what gives off the most

What questions do you have when looking at these graphs?

Reading Data with a Keen Eye

When used correctly, information from data can often help people make important decisions. However, data isn't always used correctly. Sometimes people *intentionally misuse* data to mislead others. And sometimes people *unintentionally misunderstand* what data can and cannot tell us. Understanding data and how it is used is essential to being an informed citizen!

Study the Graphs You See

Some graphs can be confusing and hard to understand when you first look at them. That's why it's important to ask questions and think about what you're looking at. You might ask yourself, *What information (or data) is the graph showing? What do the title and labels tell me? If there are X and Y axes, what do they show and how are they related to each other?*

Take a look at the graphs on this page. Could they be misleading? Read them carefully!

Let's look at this graph about poverty rates in the United States. When you first look at it, you might think that the poverty rate in our country jumped from 0 to 106 million in just two years. Be careful reading this graph. Look at where the Y axis starts—not at 0, but at 92 million! While our country has a surprisingly high poverty rate, this graph shows a trend over a short amount of time.

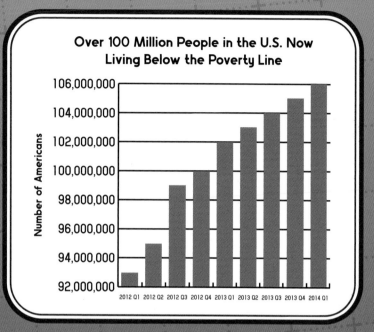

Now look at this graph about common childhood ailments. At a quick glance, you might think that 12% of all children suffer a trauma at some point when they're young. But what it really shows is that 12% of childhood ailments fall into the Trauma category. Big difference! This headline is confusing!

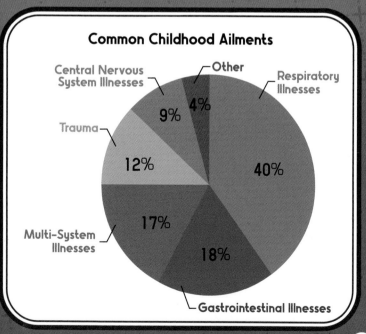

How Are Our Schools Funded?

Now that you know a little more about reading data, let's take a look at data in our schools.

? Think about your school. Do you know if it is public or private? What are some things your school has to pay for? Some common expenses are:

- Teacher and other staff salaries

- Building and playground maintenance

- Books, computers, and gym equipment

- School buses

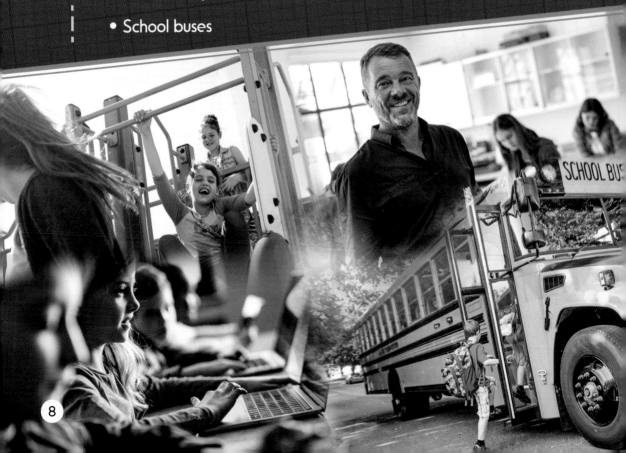

The United States has about 130,000 schools. About 100,000 of them are public schools, and the rest are private schools. Public schools are mainly paid for through taxes, while private schools are funded by other sources, like **tuition**. In this book, we focus on public schools.

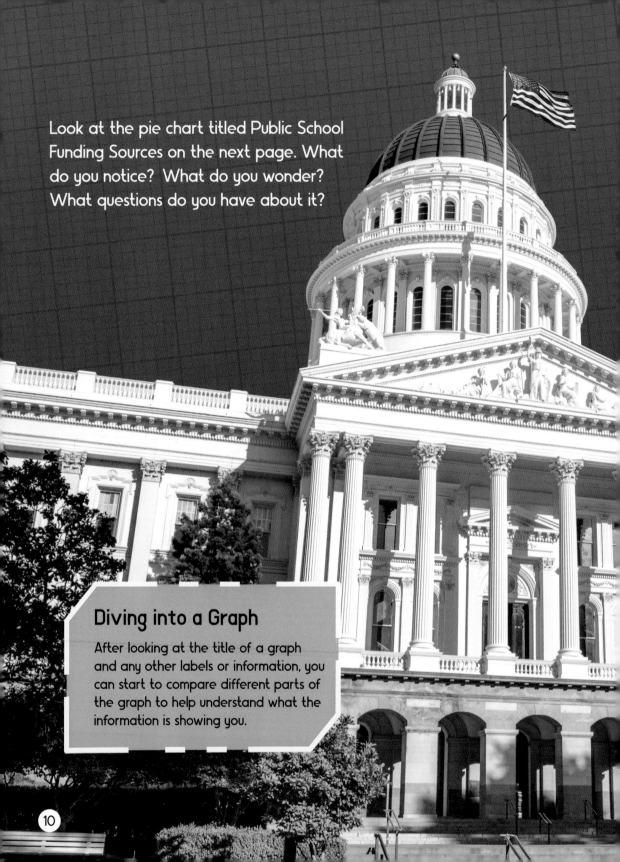

Look at the pie chart titled Public School Funding Sources on the next page. What do you notice? What do you wonder? What questions do you have about it?

Diving into a Graph

After looking at the title of a graph and any other labels or information, you can start to compare different parts of the graph to help understand what the information is showing you.

Think about these questions as you look at the pie chart:

• What data is represented in the chart?

• What does each section of the pie chart show?

• How does the amount of funding that comes from the federal government compare to the funding that comes from local property taxes?

• Many people argue that the way we fund schools is unfair. How might the data in this graph support or **refute** that argument?

Public School Funding Sources

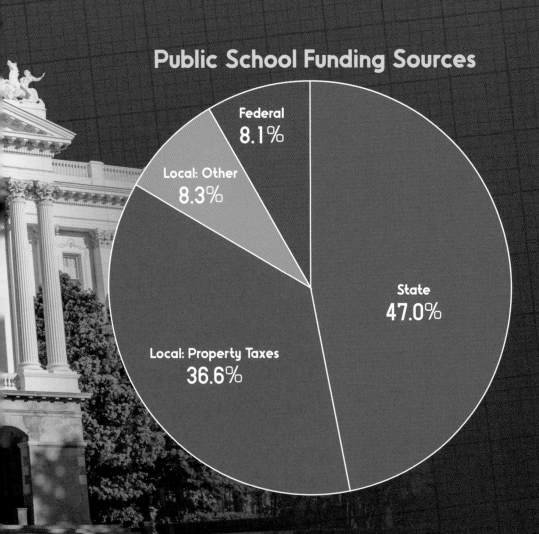

Federal
8.1%

Local: Other
8.3%

State
47.0%

Local: Property Taxes
36.6%

This pie chart shows how public schools across the United States are funded. The actual percentages for each source for any particular state or school may vary.

Public School Funding Sources

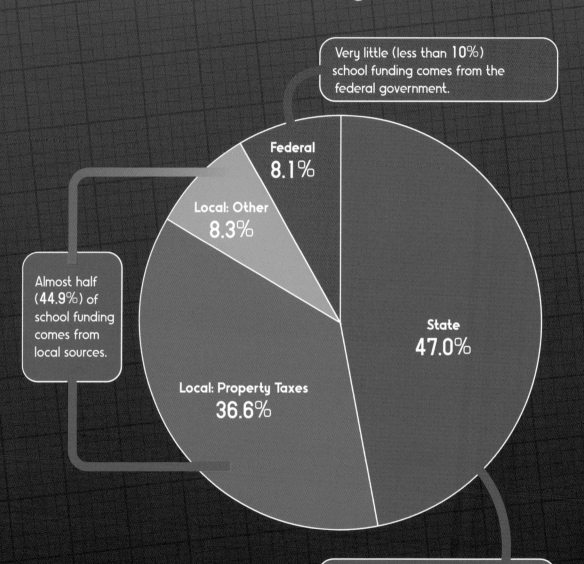

Very little (less than 10%) school funding comes from the federal government.

Federal
8.1%

Local: Other
8.3%

Almost half (44.9%) of school funding comes from local sources.

State
47.0%

Local: Property Taxes
36.6%

The largest source of school funding comes from the state. It is just slightly higher than the amount that comes from local sources.

Notice that there are four main sources for school funding. Looking at the chart, can you tell where the largest amount of money for schools comes from? The largest slice of the pie tells us that most money for schools comes from the state government. In many states, people and businesses pay taxes on the money they earn and things they buy, and some of this goes toward funding public schools within the state.

What is the next largest source of money for schools? If you said property taxes, you are right. People and businesses pay taxes to the local government on the homes, buildings, and land they own. The amount of property taxes paid depends on how much money the property is worth.

Many people feel that it is unfair that such a large portion of school funding comes from property taxes. Why? Areas with large, successful businesses and neighborhoods with expensive homes collect more money in property taxes. This means they will have more money to spend on school expenses, like newer buildings, better materials and technology, and higher teacher salaries. What is your opinion? Is it fair? Is it unfair? Why?

Ruling Says "Unfair," but Nothing Has Changed

Over 20 years ago, the Ohio Supreme Court ruled that the way that schools were funded in Ohio was unfair (DeRolph vs. State), but the inequalities in funding have not yet been fixed.

Who Goes to Our Schools?

In the fall of 2020, there were about 56.4 million (56,400,000) students across the United States. About 50.7 million of them attended public schools. To better understand the make-up of our public schools, researchers often collect data on the race and ethnicity of the students enrolled. Once collected, they analyze the data to see how the **diversity** of our school systems is changing.

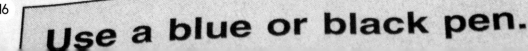

United States **Census 2020**

Use a blue or black pen.

Think about the students in your own school and in your own class. Who are they, in terms of age, gender, race/ethnicity, and other important markers of diversity?

Look at the stacked bar graph on the next page. It shows how many students of different racial/ethnic groups were enrolled in public schools in 2000, 2018, and an estimate for 2029. What do you notice? What do you wonder? What questions do you have?

Graphs Are a Valuable Visual Aid

Graphs are powerful tools we can use to show data. They allow us to **represent** large amounts of data in a visual format that is easier to read and understand. The three most common types are line graphs, bar graphs, and pie charts.

Think about these questions as you look at the bar graph:

- What do the different colors and labels at the bottom stand for?
- What does the length of each bar represent?
- Can you tell how many students of each race there were in 2000, 2018, and will be in 2029?
- Think about yourself, your friends, and other students you know. Would they be represented in this graph? Why or why not?

Enrollment in Public Schools by Race/Ethnicity

2000

2018

2029
(Projected)

| 0 | 10 | 20 | 30 | 40 | 50 | 60 |
| million | million | million | million | million | million | million |

Enrollment

- White
- Black
- Hispanic
- Asian
- Pacific Islander
- American Indian & Alaska Native
- Two or More Races

How We Think About Race and Ethnicity

Before we analyze the data in the graph, it's important to talk about the terms used for race and ethnicity. These are complex ideas, and people think about them in many ways. Sometimes the ways people think about themselves do not line up with how the government collects data about people. For example, the graph on page 19 uses the term *Hispanic*, which mainly refers to whether someone (or their ancestors) speaks Spanish or identifies with Spanish culture. However, people in this group may use other terms to identify themselves, like *Mexican American*, *Colombian*, or more broadly as *Latino*.

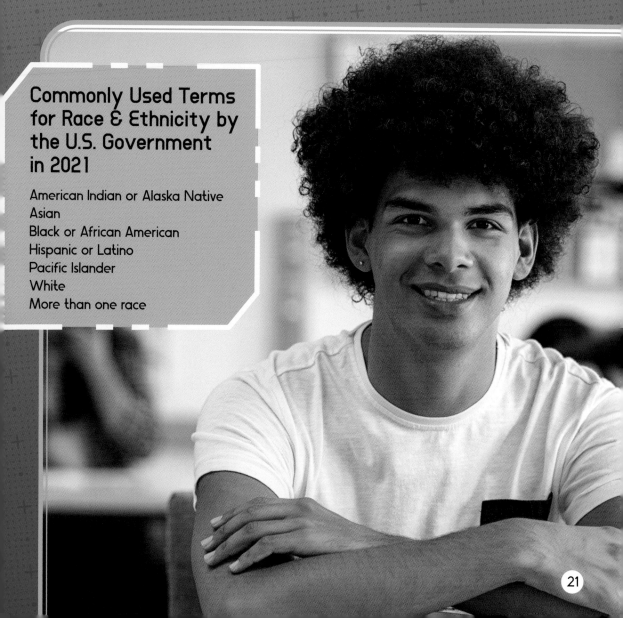

Some people identify as both Black and Hispanic or White and Hispanic. Different data sources count these people differently. Some data sources include people who identify like this in both categories (for example, counting them under Black students and Hispanic students). Other data sources (like this one) only include them under the category of Hispanic. Our graph shows the terms/categories that are most often used by the United States government.

Commonly Used Terms for Race & Ethnicity by the U.S. Government in 2021

American Indian or Alaska Native
Asian
Black or African American
Hispanic or Latino
Pacific Islander
White
More than one race

21

Perhaps most importantly, the way we view and understand race and ethnicity has more to do with our thinking than it does with a scientific method of categorizing people. Like our society, the language we use to discuss race is always evolving.

The Changing Categories of Ethnic Groups in the U.S.

The terms the government uses to define people have changed multiple times over the years, and will probably continue to change for years to come. For example, Hawaiian, Part Hawaiian, Samoan, and Guamanian used to fall under the Asian category on a census form. Now they have their own category: Pacific Islander.

Look at the graph on the next page. This graph shows the race/ethnicity of students in our country's public schools in 2000 and 2018. It also shows an estimate (or **projection**) for 2029 based on current **trends**.

Let's look at the year 2018. Altogether, there were about 51 million public school students. Each color shows how many students of each racial/ethnic group there are, but be careful when you read this graph. In a stacked bar graph, each new group starts where the other one ends. For example, there were about 8 million Black students in 2018, not 32 million.

Remember, the terms the government uses for different ethnicities have changed over time. The government didn't start collecting data about Pacific Islanders and students of two or more races until 2018. Before that, they were mixed in with other groups. How do you think this change has affected the data?

What do you notice or wonder about how enrollment is changing over time? Is your school's enrollment following these trends?

Enrollment in Public Schools by Race/Ethnicity

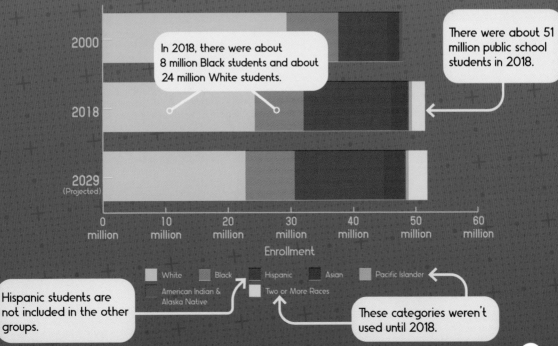

In 2018, there were about 8 million Black students and about 24 million White students.

There were about 51 million public school students in 2018.

2000

2018

2029
(Projected)

| 0 million | 10 million | 20 million | 30 million | 40 million | 50 million | 60 million |

Enrollment

White Black Hispanic Asian Pacific Islander

American Indian & Alaska Native Two or More Races

Hispanic students are not included in the other groups.

These categories weren't used until 2018.

Did you notice that the Hispanic student group is the group that grew the most from 2000 to 2018? It grew in terms of the actual number of students and also in the percentage they are of the total **student body**. If you look at the 2029 projection, how is this data expected to change in the future?

You may have also noticed that the number of Asian and **biracial**/multiracial students is increasing too. What do you notice about the White group of students? The graph shows that the number of White students in the U.S. is decreasing, both in overall number and as a percentage of the total student body.

Enrollment in Public Schools by Race/Ethnicity

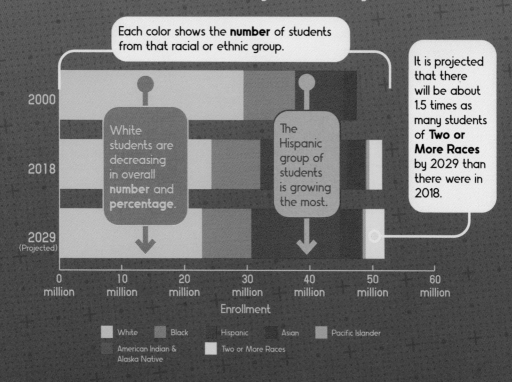

Each color shows the **number** of students from that racial or ethnic group.

White students are decreasing in overall **number** and **percentage**.

The Hispanic group of students is growing the most.

It is projected that there will be about 1.5 times as many students of **Two or More Races** by 2029 than there were in 2018.

2000

2018

2029
(Projected)

| 0 million | 10 million | 20 million | 30 million | 40 million | 50 million | 60 million |

Enrollment

White   Black   Hispanic   Asian   Pacific Islander

American Indian & Alaska Native   Two or More Races

Although the graph on the previous page shows that public schools in the United States are becoming more diverse as a whole, many neighborhoods, schools, and school districts still lack much-needed diversity. Because of this, they miss out on the advantages of a racially and ethnically diverse community, like learning about other cultures and gaining an appreciation of people different from themselves.

Diversity Is a Good Thing

With a friend or an adult, talk about the advantages of having a diverse school population.

Diversity can be measured in many ways, including race/ethnicity, gender, language, religion, socioeconomic status, and more. In what ways is your school diverse? In what ways is it not diverse? How do you feel about this? Why do you feel this way?

Who Has Internet Access?

In today's world, having access to the internet is a necessity. Most people use it every day for a variety of tasks. Do you have access to the internet at home? Who uses it the most in your home? What do they use it for? Think about your internet usage. How and where do you access the internet to do your schoolwork, play games, watch shows, and connect with others?

With Internet Access at Home, You Can Do Anything!

- Take classes and learn remotely
- Earn a college degree
- Work from home
- Research and apply for jobs
- Search for information about anything
- Read the news (local to international)
- Pay bills
- Plan and book vacations
- Communicate with long-distance friends and family
- Watch shows, movies, and concerts
- And much more!

While many students can access the internet from home to complete their schoolwork, not everyone can. Students without internet access at home often have to use the internet at school, the public library, or other places in their community to get their work done. What kind of challenges does this present? Does this put those students at a disadvantage? Why or why not?

Access to the Internet Is Not Equal

Quality of internet access may depend on where someone lives. For example, urban and suburban areas often have faster, better, and less expensive internet access than rural areas.

Look at the bar graph about home internet access on the next page. What do you notice? What do you wonder? What questions do you have?

? Think about these questions as you look at the bar graph:

- What do the horizontal and vertical axes represent?

- Think about yourself, your friends, and other students you know. Would they be represented in this graph? Why or why not?

- In what ways might this graph not tell the "whole story" about students' home internet access?

Percentage of 3- to 18-Year-Olds Who Had Home Internet Access in 2018, by Child's Race/Ethnicity

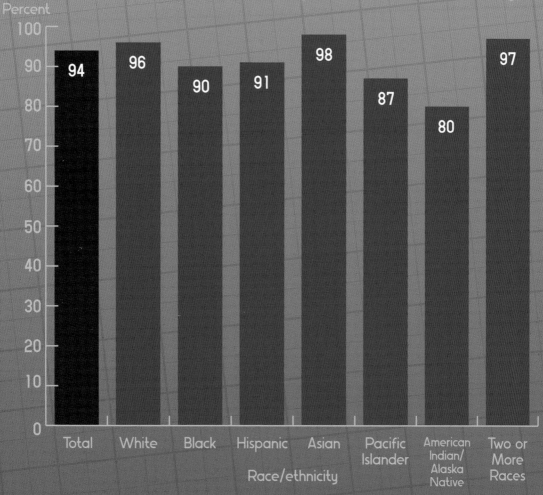

NOTE 1: Total includes other racial/ethnic groups not shown separately.

NOTE 2: Includes only 3- to 18-year-olds living in households. Respondents living in group quarters, such as shelters, healthcare facilities, or correctional facilities, were not asked about internet access.

NOTE 3: Race categories exclude persons of Hispanic ethnicity.

What did you wonder and notice about the data related to home internet access?

At first glance, you might notice that the overwhelming majority (a whopping 94% of children ages 3 to 18 years old) had access to the internet at home in 2018. But when you look closer, you'll see that not every group experiences such high **connectivity**.

Percentage of 3- to 18-Year-Olds Who Had Home Internet Access in 2018, by Child's Race/Ethnicity

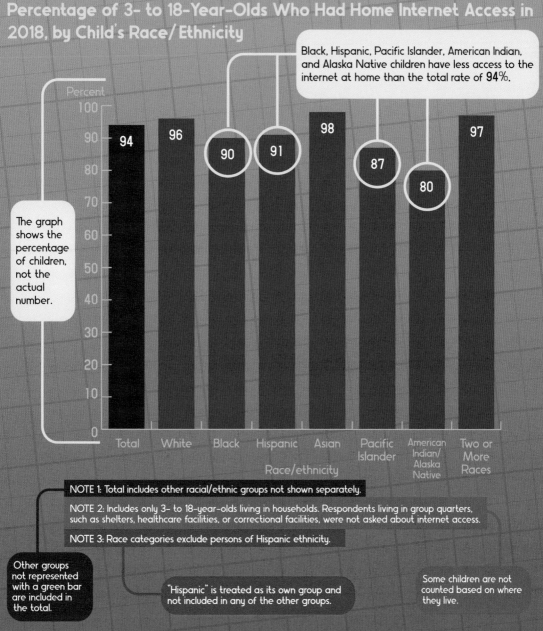

Black, Hispanic, Pacific Islander, American Indian, and Alaska Native children have less access to the internet at home than the total rate of **94%**.

The graph shows the percentage of children, not the actual number.

NOTE 1: Total includes other racial/ethnic groups not shown separately.

NOTE 2: Includes only 3- to 18-year-olds living in households. Respondents living in group quarters, such as shelters, healthcare facilities, or correctional facilities, were not asked about internet access.

NOTE 3: Race categories exclude persons of Hispanic ethnicity.

Other groups not represented with a green bar are included in the total.

"Hispanic" is treated as its own group and not included in any of the other groups.

Some children are not counted based on where they live.

When comparing the data, we see that four racial/ethnic groups have less access to the internet than the total rate of 94%. Only three groups have a higher rate of access. What questions does this raise for you? Is this fair?

The notes at the bottom help complete the "story" behind the chart.

What This Graph Does NOT Show Us

While this graph shows that most groups had high rates of internet access at home, it does not include data about the quality of the internet connection. During the COVID-19 pandemic, many families suddenly found that they had to rely on the internet more than ever before for school and work, and this uncovered problems with their internet. Many discovered that their connection wasn't fast enough or reliable enough. Because of this, they had to find access elsewhere: at their public library (if it was open), doing schoolwork in their school's parking lot to access the school's Wi-Fi, or checking out a temporary mobile hotspot device from their library to use at home. While these worked in a pinch, none of these solutions even come close to having a fast, reliable connection at home whenever it is needed.

The data tells you that 94% of 3- to 18-year-olds have access to the internet, right? But how might this data be misleading? Remember that only three of the seven racial/ethnic groups represented have more than 94%. Is it good for society that more than half of the represented groups have a lower rate of access to the internet? How could someone be misled by the total percentage of 94%?

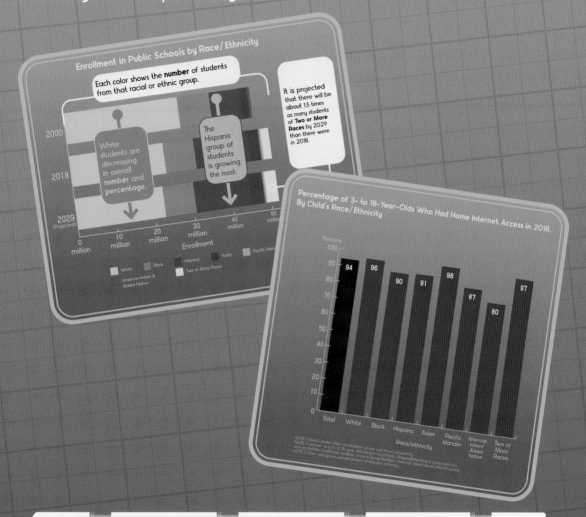

Combining Data for More Meaning

The White group, which has had declining enrollment since 2000, is one of the three groups with a high internet access rate. The Hispanic group, which has had increasing enrollment since 2000, is one of the four with a lower internet access rate. What could be some consequences of this?

Using Data to Uncover Inequality

Now that we have explored some data related to schools, think about what you have wondered and noticed as you've looked at the data in the graphs and charts. Does any of the data surprise you? Does any of it bother you?

Sometimes data can shed light on **injustices** in our society. It can uncover inequalities that we didn't know existed. Think about what the data has shown you about school funding and property taxes. What injustices in funding might this data show?

When data shows consistent differences in outcomes for different racial and/or ethnic groups, like we saw with the Home Internet Access chart, it is evidence of systemic **racism**.

What is racism? People define racism in different ways. Many people define racism as **bias** against someone because of the color of their skin. However, most researchers understand racism as a society-wide force that creates advantages for some groups while also creating disadvantages for other groups.

Data that illustrates injustices can sometimes be uncomfortable for people to learn about and think about. Whether someone has experienced injustice firsthand or not, the idea of people or groups of people being treated unfairly based on age, gender, or race/ethnicity can be unsettling.

For some people, the data reminds them of difficulties that they, their friends, or their family have experienced, and it may make them angry. They may also feel powerless in trying to change things.

When faced with injustice, people may feel like they want to do something about it, but they don't know what.

Here are a few ideas of how someone could turn those feelings into actions of positive change:

- Start a conversation about it with friends or family.

- Research the topic to educate themselves on it.

- Post true and accurate information from reputable sources on social media to educate others and start a conversation.

- Join a local organization/group that focuses on the inequality.

- Write to a local government official about the inequality and suggest changes or actions that can be made to reverse it.

Sometimes people are angered when the data shows they have advantages in a particular area. They think about the challenges they have faced in life and how they have worked hard to get where they are. You or those you know may have overcome great challenges, and you should be proud of that. At the same time, in some areas other people may have faced additional challenges because of the color of their skin, the amount of money they have, their gender, or other aspects of who they are.

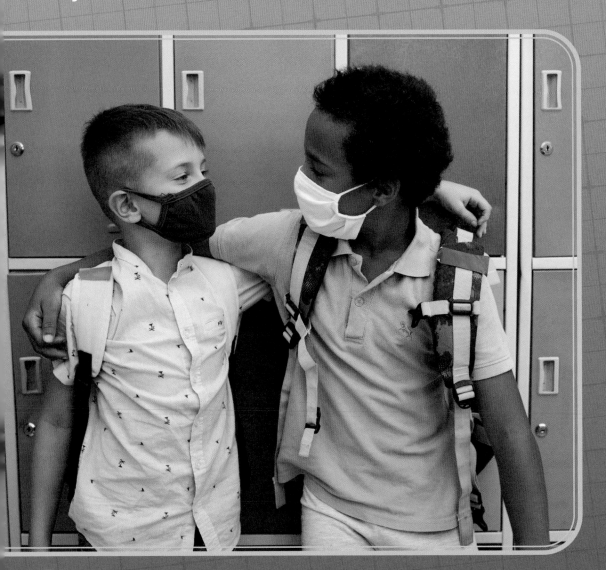

Data is just one tool we have to help us understand our world and our schools. Valuable data shown in graphs and charts can help people make informed decisions, understand inequalities right around us, and change the world to make it a better place. When used to inform and educate others, data can make change happen!

Questions for Reflection

Let's connect data to your life. Answer the following questions and record your answers in a notebook.

1. How do you or your family use data in your everyday life?

2. What is some data you could collect about your friends? About students in your classroom? About students in your school? How would you collect it?

3. What injustices do you see in your world, and how could data help you better understand them?

4. What can you do to challenge the injustices that you see?

Extension Activity

Informed citizens learn how to find, analyze, and discuss data about our world. Now it's your turn to find and analyze data on a topic that interests you.

1. Choose a topic related to education that you want to know more about.

2. See what data and graphs you can find about your topic in news articles or on the internet.

3. Find one or more graphs about your topic and analyze what they are showing you:

    a. Can you explain the data the graph is showing?

    b. What comparisons can you make within the graph?

    c. How does this apply to the real world?

4. Share what you found with a friend or an adult. Ask each other questions about the graph and what it means.

Glossary

bias (BYE-uhs): to favor or oppose a particular group or person

biracial (BYE-RAY-shuhl): of, relating to, or involving members of two races

connectivity (kuh-NEK-tiv-i-tee): the ability to connect to or communicate with another computer

diversity (di-VUR-si-tee): a variety

injustice (in-JUHS-tis): unfairness or lack of justice

projection (pruh-JEK-shuhn): an estimate or a prediction

racism (RAY-sis-m): the systemic oppression of a racial group to the social, economic, and political advantage of another

refute (ree-FYOOT): to prove wrong by argument or evidence

represent (rep-ri-ZENT): to be a sign or symbol of something

student body (STOO-duhnt BAH-dee): the students in a school

trends (trendz): the general direction in which things are developing

tuition (too-ISH-uhn): money paid to a college or private school in order for a student to study there

Index

Bibliography

Arbel, Tali, "'Big Burden' for Schools Trying to Give Kids Internet Access." *AP News*. https://apnews.com/article/joe-biden-us-news-distance-learning-coronavirus-pandemic-internet-access-94c57075af6a3d539abe78bbb7e934ce (accessed April 11, 2021).

Curcio, Frances R., "Developing Data-Graph Comprehension in Grades K–8 (3rd edition)." National Council of Teachers of Mathematics.

National Center for Education Statistics, "Fast Facts: Educational Institutions." https://nces.ed.gov/fastfacts/display.asp?id=84 (accessed May 4, 2021).

National Center for Education Statistics, "Elementary and Secondary Education." https://nces.ed.gov/programs/digest/d19/ch_2.asp.

National Center for Education Statistics, "Public School Revenue Sources." The Condition of Education. https://nces.ed.gov/programs/coe/indicator_cma.asp, (accessed April 11, 2021).

National Center for Education Statistics, "Table 235.10 Revenues for public elementary and secondary schools, by source of funds: Selected years, 1919–20 through 2016–17." 2019 Digest of Education Statistics. https://nces.ed.gov/programs/digest/d19/tables/dt19_235.10.asp, (accessed April 11, 2021).

National Center for Education Statistics, "Children's Internet Access at Home." The Condition of Education. https://nces.ed.gov/programs/coe/indicator_cch.asp, (accessed April 11, 2021).

National Center for Education Statistics, "Racial/Ethnic Enrollment in Public Schools." The Condition of Education. https://nces.ed.gov/programs/coe/indicator_cge.asp, (accessed April 11, 2021).

National Center for Education Statistics, "Table 203.50. Enrollment and percentage distribution of enrollment in public elementary and secondary schools, by race/ethnicity and region: Selected years, fall 1995 through fall 2029." 2020 Digest of Education Statistics. https://nces.ed.gov/programs/digest/d20/tables/dt20_203.50.asp, (accessed April 11, 2021).

About the Authors

Courtney Koestler and Matt Felton–Koestler live in Athens, Ohio, where they are faculty members in the Department of Teacher Education in the Patton College of Education at Ohio University. They like to spend time with their kid, Parker, and their cat, Bitsy, and spend time outdoors with their friends.

Photos by Ben Siegel, Ohio University Photographer

www.rourkeeducationalmedia.com

PHOTO CREDITS: cover, page 1: diane39/ Getty Images; cover, page 1: traffic_analyzer/ Getty Images; page 4: gorodenkoff/ Getty Images; page 5: JINGXUAN JI/ Getty Images; page 6: By Antonio Guillem/ Shutterstock.com; page 8: skynesher/Getty Images; page 8: stu99/ Getty Images; page 8: martinedoucet/ Getty Images; page 8: Ridofranz/ Getty Images; page 9: Wavebreakmedia/ Getty Images; page 9: monkeybusinessimages/Getty Images; page 10: dszc/ Getty Images; page 13: BrianAJackson/Getty Images; page 14: photovs/ Getty Images; page 15: AlfonsoTerry/ Getty Images; page 15: AzmanL/ Getty Images; page 16: liveslow/ Getty Images; page 17: gradyreese/ Getty Images; page 18: kali9/ Getty Images; page 19: FatCamera/ Getty Images; page 20: PhotoInc/ Getty Images; page 21: Ridofranz/ Getty Images; page 22: YinYang/ Getty Images; page 23: SolStock/ Getty Images; page 24: SDI Productions/ Getty Images; page 25: kali9/ Getty Images; page 26: Feverpitched/ Getty Images; page 27: Ridofranz/ Getty Images; page 28: Pollyana Ventura/ Getty Images; page 29: chameleonseye/ Getty Images; page 29: martinedoucet/ Getty Images; page 29: NicolasMcComber/ Getty Images; page 29: JamesBrey/ Getty Images; page 30: insta_photos/ Getty Images; page 31: Phynart Studio/ Getty Images; page 31: AJ_Watt/ Getty Images; page 31: LeoPatrizi/ Getty Images; page 31: franckreporter/ Getty Images; page 32: Sasha_Suzi/ Getty Images; page 34: fizkes/ Getty Images; page 36: eyecrave/ Getty Images; page 37: Milko/ Getty Images; page 37: piyaset/ Getty Images; page 38: CAP53/ Getty Images; page 38: Motortion/ Getty Images; page 39: Anastasiia Yanishevska/ Getty Images; page 40: LeoPatrizi/ Getty Images; page 41: Daisy-Daisy/ Getty Images; page 42: FluxFactory/ Getty Images; page 43: da-kuk/ Getty Images; page 43: Plyushkin/ Getty Images; page 44: 4x6/ Getty Images;

Library of Congress PCN Data

Exploring Our Schools / Koestler, Felton-Koestler
(Data In Your World)
ISBN 9781-7-3165-174-7 (hard cover)
ISBN 9781-7-3165-219-5 (soft cover)
ISBN 9781-7-3165-189-1 (e-Book)
ISBN 9781-7-3165-204-1 (epub)
Library of Congress Control Number: 2021944585

Rourke Educational Media
Printed in the United States of America
01-0462211937

Edited by: **Cary Malaski**
Cover and interior design by: **J.J. Giddings**